SWASTICK BOOK BOX
MASON OF WINNERS

SBB

Cursive
WRITING BOOK
Small Letters

Awesome Cursive Writing Practice Book for Kids

By: **Preeti Garg**

AF516963

Follow the patterns with your pencil.

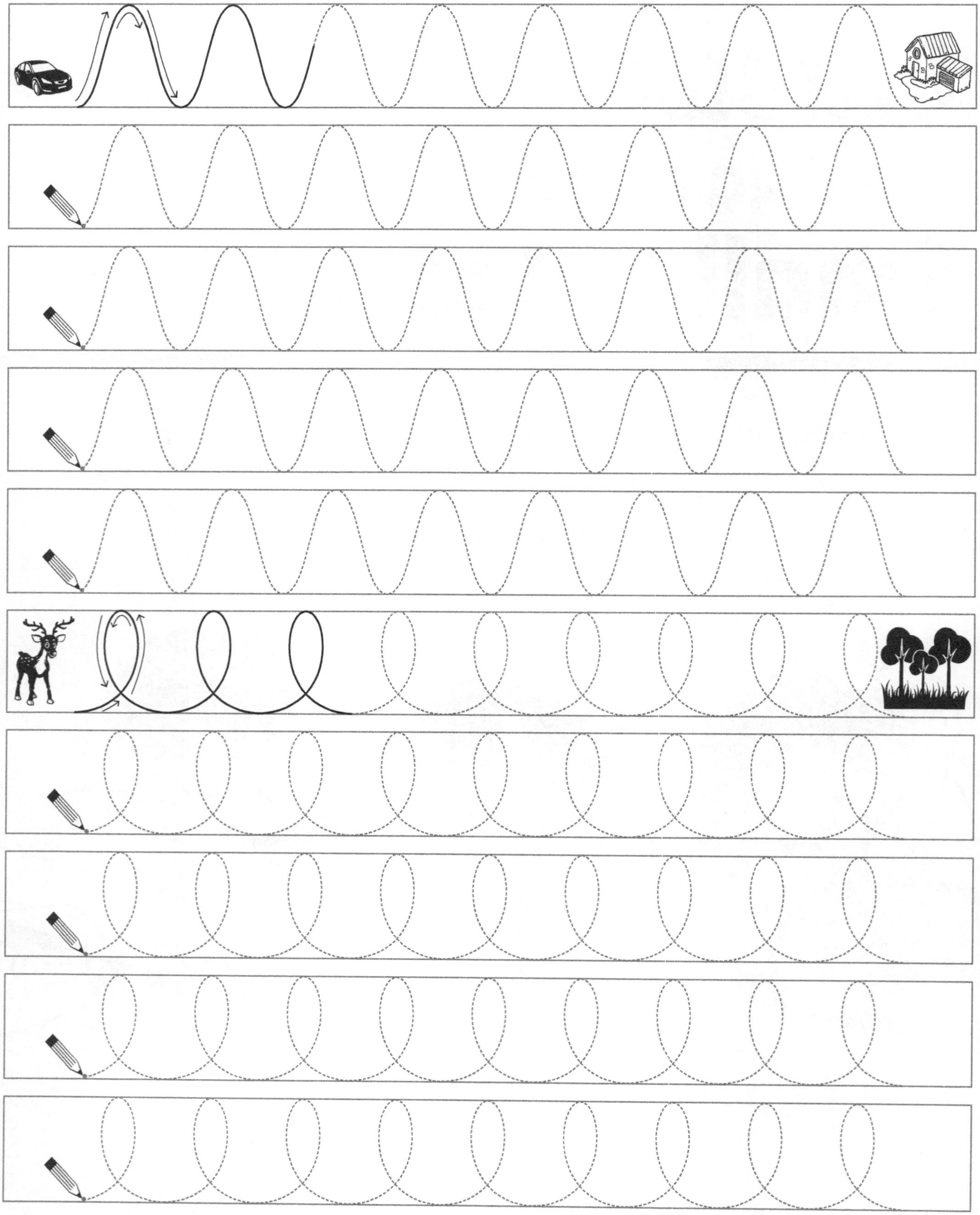

Date : ....

Teacher's Signature : ....

Follow the patterns with your pencil.

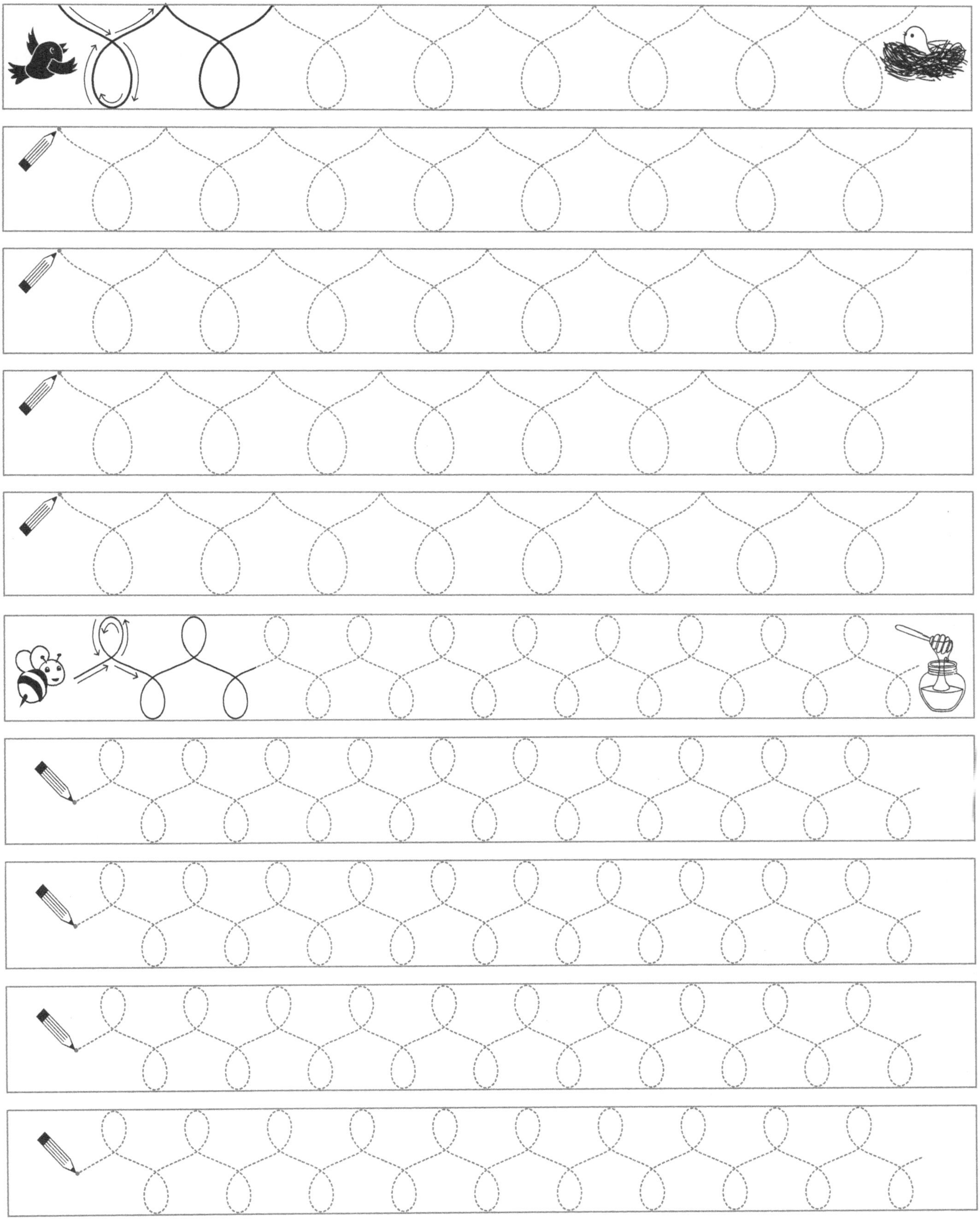

Date : ....

Teacher's Signature : ....

apple

Date : ....

Teacher's Signature : ....

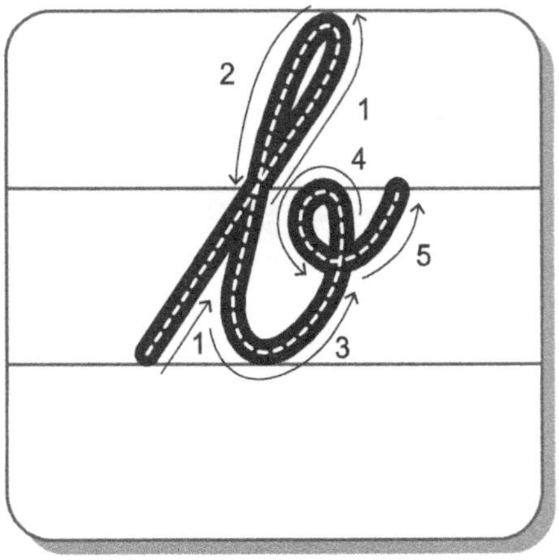

ball

car

Date : ....

Teacher's Signature : ....

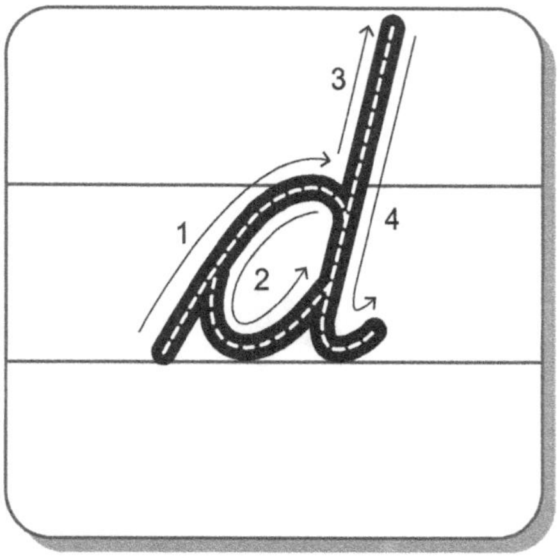

dog

d	d	d	d	d	d	d
d	d	d	d	d	d	d
d	d	d	d	d	d	d
d	d	d	d	d	d	d
d	d	d	d	d	d	d
d	d	d	d	d	d	d
d	d	d	d	d	d	d

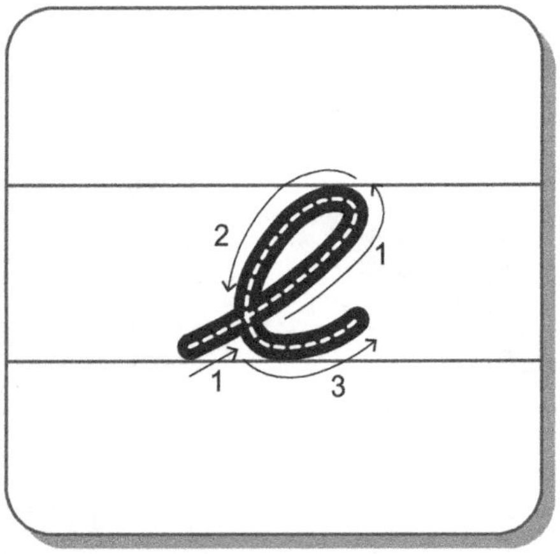

elephant

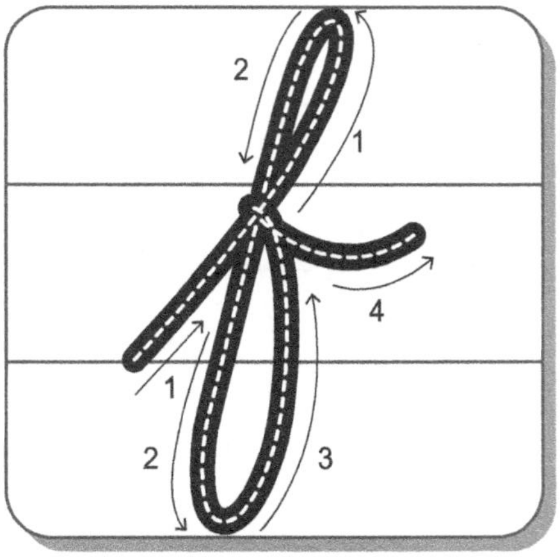

fish

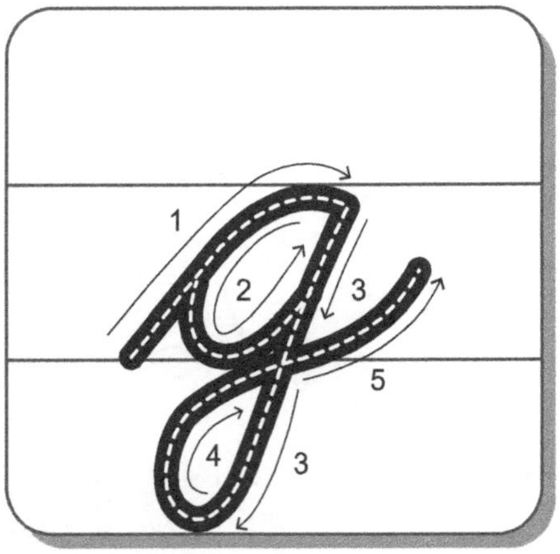

grapes

Date : ....

Teacher's Signature : ....

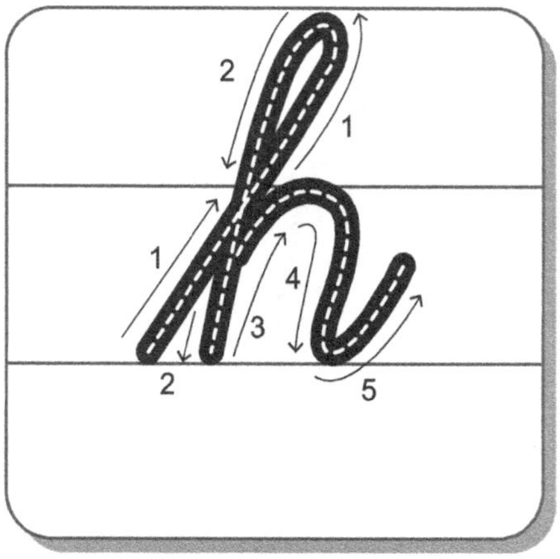

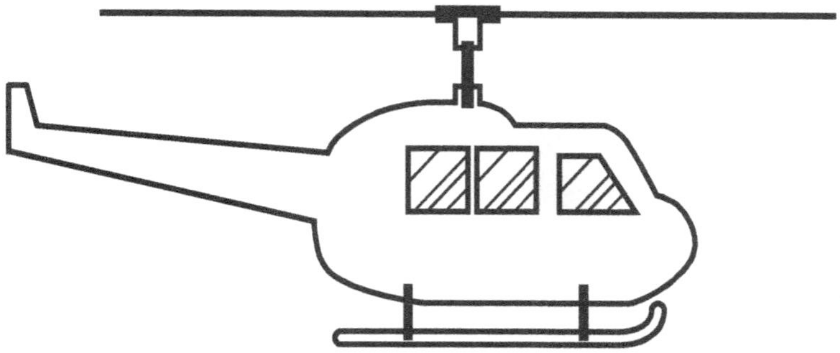

helicopter

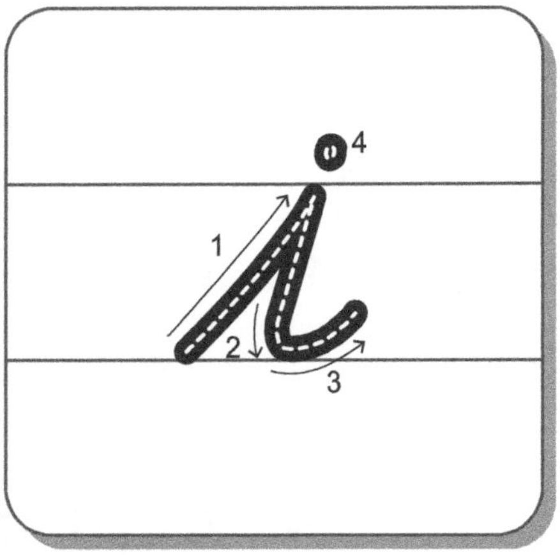

igloo

i	i	i	i	i	i	i
i	i	i	i	i	i	i
i	i	i	i	i	i	i
i	i	i	i	i	i	i
i	i	i	i	i	i	i
i	i	i	i	i	i	i
i	i	i	i	i	i	i

Date : ....

Teacher's Signature : ....

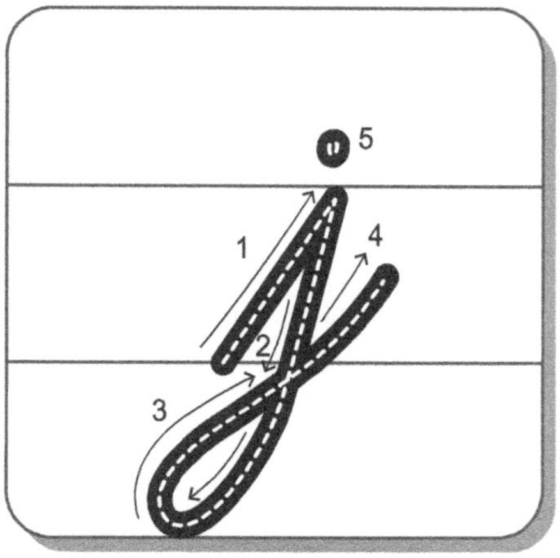

jug

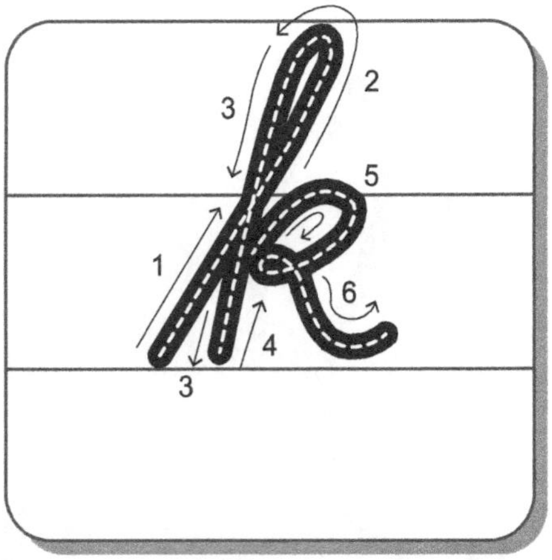

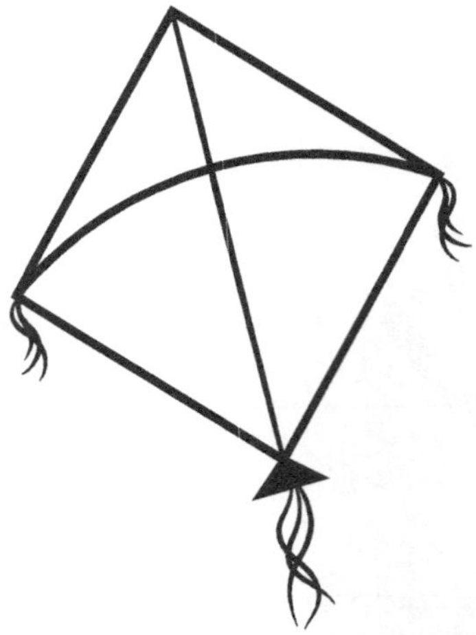

kite

Date : ....

Teacher's Signature : ....

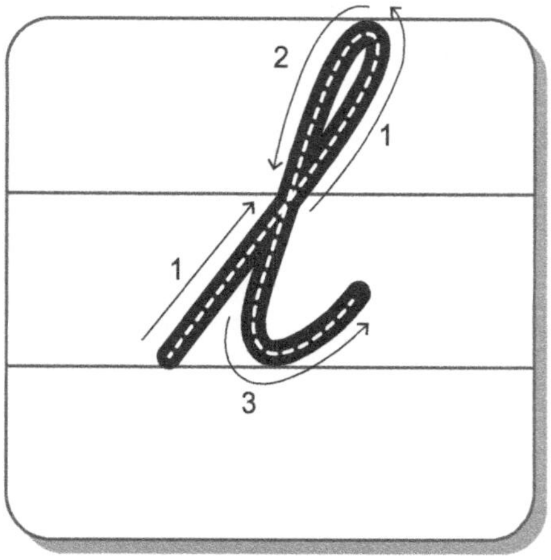

lock

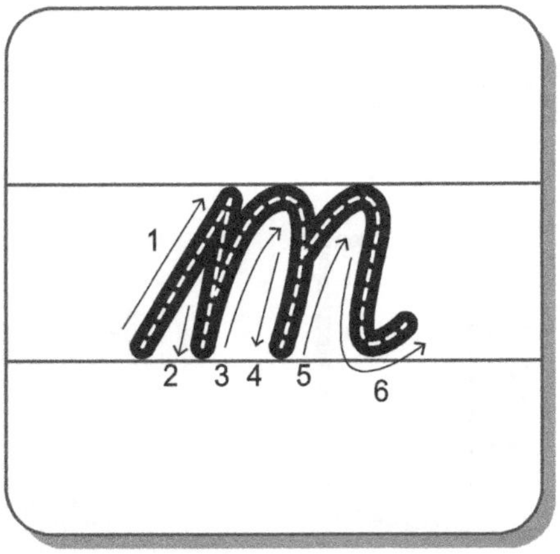

Mango

Date : ....

Teacher's Signature : ....

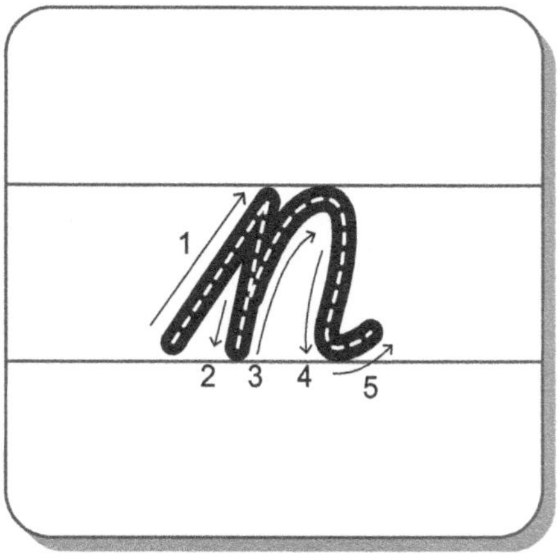

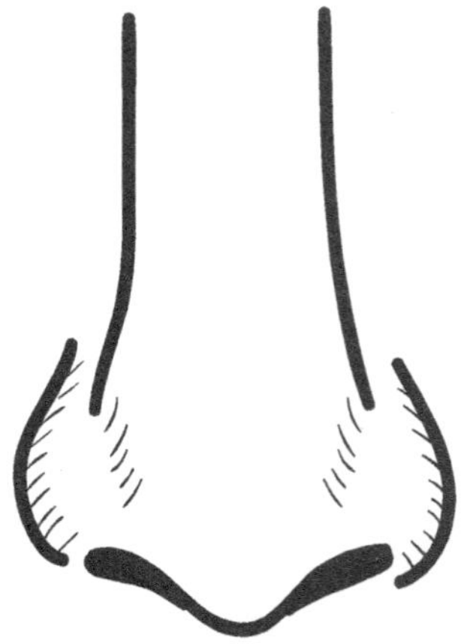

nose

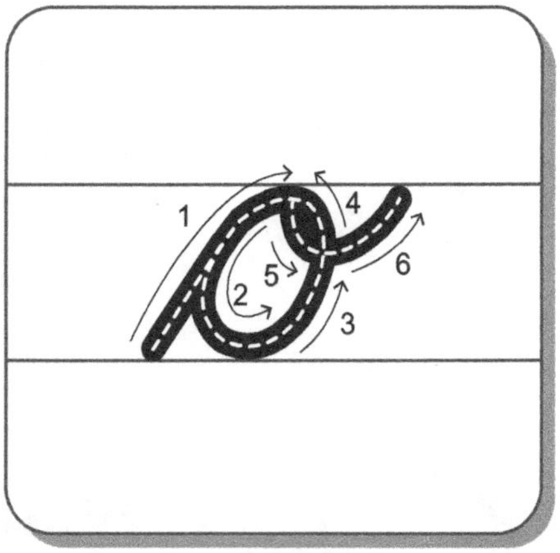

orange

pencil

Date : ....

Teacher's Signature : ....

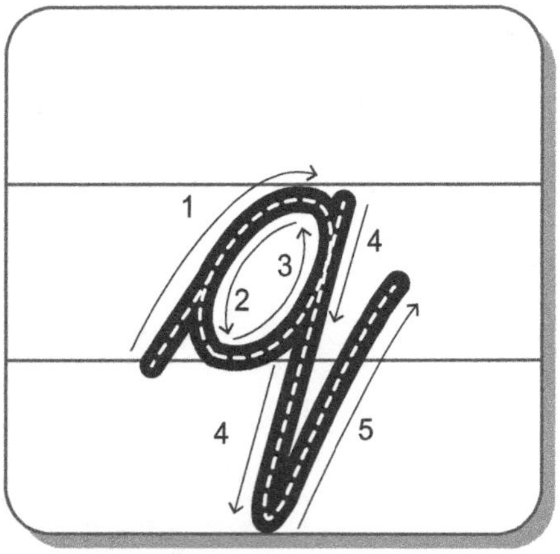

quill

Date : ....

Teacher's Signature : ....

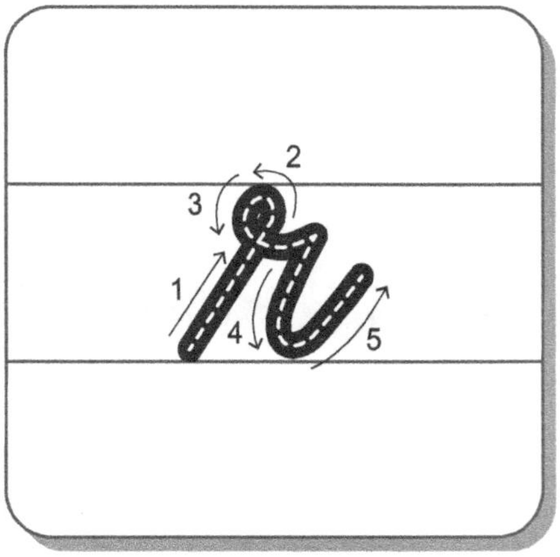

rat

r r r r r r r

r r r r r r r

r r r r r r r

r r r r r r r

r r r r r r r

r r r r r r r

r r r r r r r

Date : ....

Teacher's Signature : ....

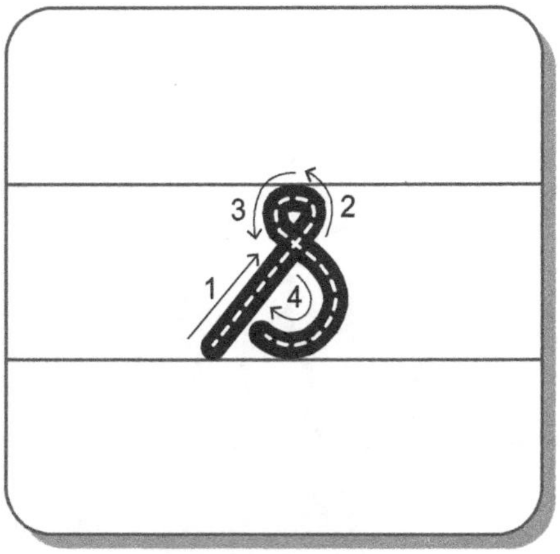

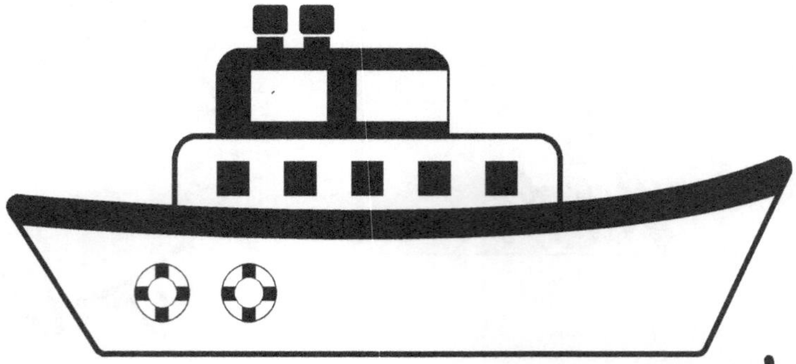

ship

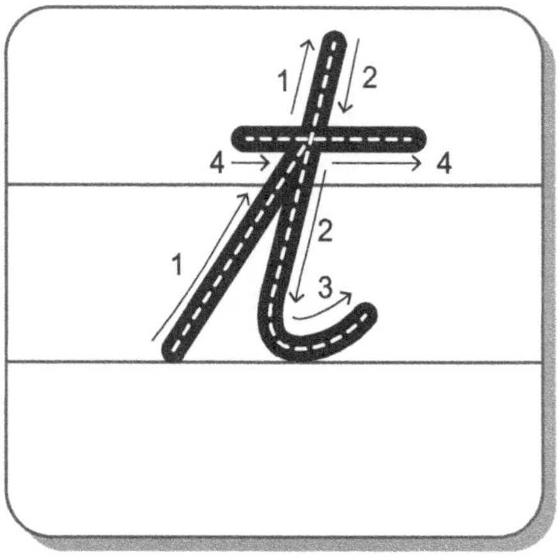

top

Date : ....

Teacher's Signature : ....

umbrella

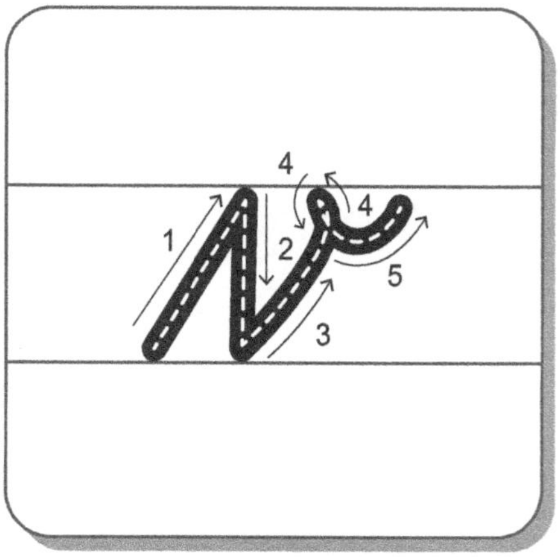

van

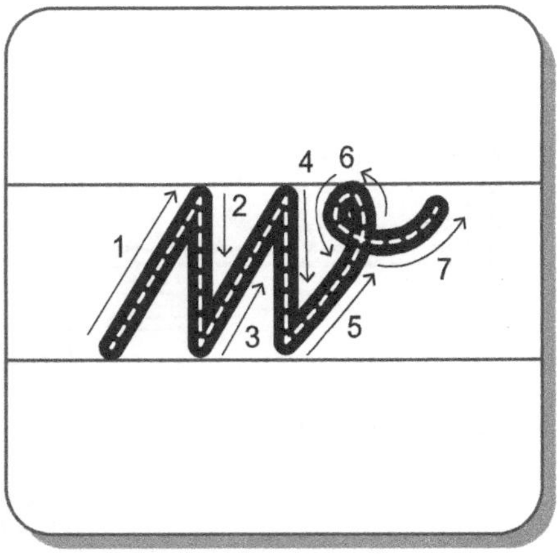

watch

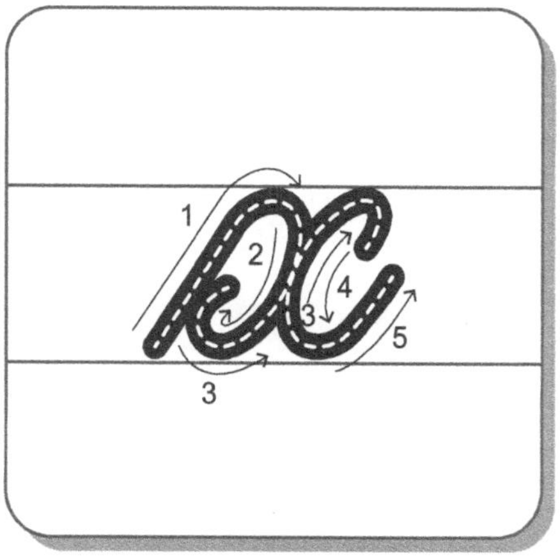

x-mas tree

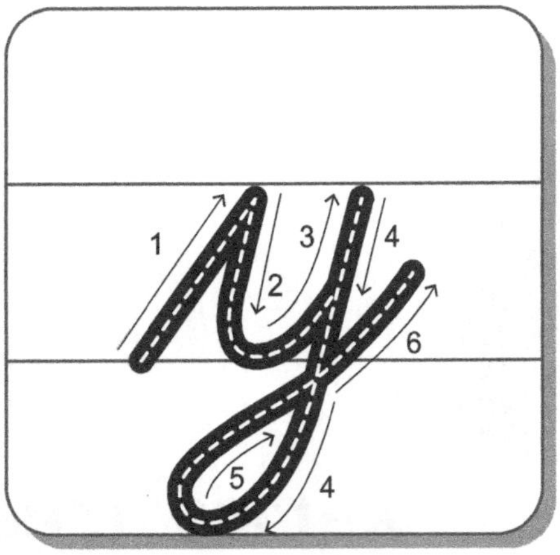

yacht

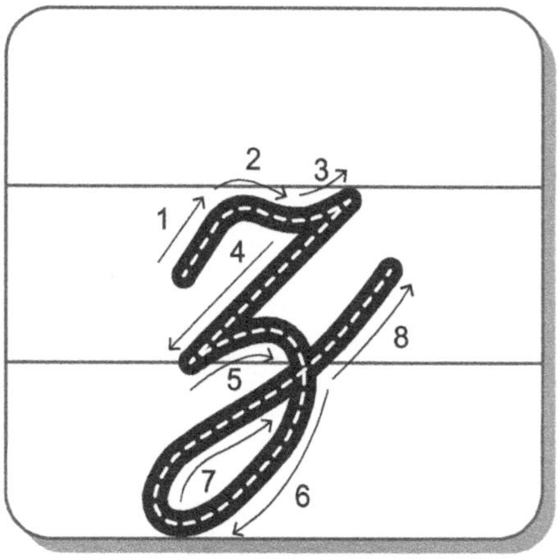

zebra

Date : ....

Teacher's Signature : ....

Say and trace the letters.

a	b	c	d	e	f
g	h	i	j	k	l
m	n	o	p	q	r
s	t	u	v	w	x
y	z				

Write the letters a to z.

Write the missing letters from a to z.

a	b		d	e	
g		i	j		
m		o	p		r
s	t		v		x
	z				

Write the letter that comes after the given letter.

g		b		o	
m		i		r	

Write the letter that comes before the given letter.

	z		t		v
	p		o		e

Date : ....

Teacher's Signature : ....

Match and write the letters with objects they start with.

O

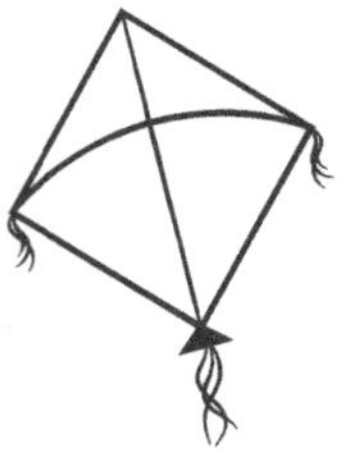

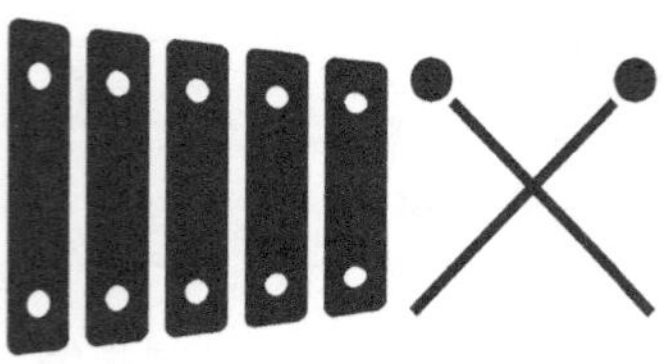